Prayers on the Go
Finding Peace in Difficult Times

Joan M. Blake

Copyright © 2019 by Joan M. Blake
All rights reserved.

No part of this publication may be reproduced in any form or by any means, electronic or mechanical, including photocopy, recording, or any information or retrieval system, without written permission from the author.

ISBN: 978-0-9814609-7-0

Published by
Key to Life Publishing Company
P.O. Box 190971
Boston, MA 02119
keytolifepublishingcompany.com

Unless otherwise indicated, Scriptures are taken from the Holy Bible, New International Version® (NIV®): Copyright ©1973, 1978, 1984, 2011 by Biblica, Inc.®, 1820 Jet Stream Drive, Colorado Springs, CO 80921. Used by permission. All rights reserved worldwide.

Scriptures taken from the New King James Version®: Copyright © 1982 by Thomas Nelson Bibles, P.O. Box 141000, Nashville, TN 37214. Used by permission. All rights reserved.

Scriptures taken from the Living Bible: Copyright © 1971 by Tyndale House Foundation. Used by permission of Tyndale House Publishers Inc., 351 Executive Drive, Carol Stream, IL 60188. All rights reserved.

Printed in the United States of America

Dedication

I dedicate this book to our son Karl, a committed husband and father of two children. I pray that he will find *Prayers on the Go: Finding Peace in Difficult Times* useful, fulfilling and inspirational.

Acknowledgements

I acknowledge my husband Carl, our two sons Karl and Maurice, our daughters Leah and Emily, and their spouses for their love, continued support, and encouragement.

I thank Dianne Lashley, my prayer partner, for suggesting the title of the book, and my other prayer partners, friends, and extended family members, for their prayers and support over the years.

I thank God for His love, compassion, faithfulness, and healing power. He is a Mighty God, worthy of all praise and adoration. With God's help I can advance against a troop; with my God I can scale a wall *(Psalm 18:29)*. With Him, all things are possible *(Matthew 19:26)*.

Introduction

I wrote Prayers on the Go: *Finding Peace in Difficult Times*, to affirm God's love and faithfulness toward you. He loves you regardless of who you are, how you feel about yourself or what you have done; He is with you in your most difficult moments and promises never to leave or forsake you. With open arms of forgiveness, God waits for you, His sons or daughters, who are willing to confess and repent of your wrongdoings and accept Jesus, His Son, as your Lord and Savior.

I have carefully designed these 31 prayers for anyone needing prayer, for women and men who are experiencing emotional pain from their past, and who need a dose of comfort each day; for women and men who need a taste of God's love while traveling to and from work, and on their lunch breaks; and lastly, for the busy mom or dad who cares for loved ones at home and needs daily encouragement.

I, too, am a mother dealing with an adult daughter with special needs, and although I have experienced difficult times, God continues to comfort me, carry me, and give me hope. I encourage you to keep your faith alive by reaching out to God with a renewed heart and mind, and with hands uplifted to receive miracles, signs, and wonders from Him. God cares for you; He hears your prayers and bears your burdens. He is faithful who has called you and will do these things *(1 Thessalonians 5:24)*.

Table of Contents

Introduction .... page III

Prayer 1 Prayer of Affirmation of Who I Am .... page 1

Prayer 2 Prayer for Salvation .... page 2

Prayer 3 Prayer to Increase One's Faith .... page 3

Prayer 4 Prayer to Cease from Lying, Stealing, or Other Wrongdoings .... page 4

Prayer 5 Prayer of Forgiveness .... page 5

Prayer 6 Prayer to Love Others .... page 6

Prayer 7 Prayer to Overcome Fear .... page 7

Prayer 8 Prayer to Overcome Jealousy or Gossip .... page 8

Prayer 9 Prayer to Overcome Anger or Guilt .... page 9

Prayer 10 Prayer for Healing .... page 10

Prayer 11 Prayer to Overcome Procrastination .... page 11

Prayer 12 Prayer to Overcome My Past .... page 12

Prayer 13 Prayer when Experiencing Anxiety, Loneliness, and Self-Pity .... page 13

Prayer 14 Prayer for My Spouse .... page 14

Prayer 15 Prayer of Repentance .... page 15

Prayer 16 Prayer for Protection While Traveling .... page 16

Prayer 17 Prayer for Wisdom and Understanding .... page 17

Prayer 18 Prayer to Be Successful in Leadership .... page 18

Prayer 19 Prayer for a Single Parent .... page 19

Prayer 20 Prayer for Patience While Seeking a Job .... page 20

Prayer 21 Prayer for Healing from Drinking, Smoking
or Drugs .... page 21

Prayer 22 Prayer for an Individual Dealing with Bipolar, Schizo-
phrenia, Anorexia, Bulimia and Other Disorders ... page 22

Prayer 23 Prayer for Parent(s) Who Lost a Son or Daughter
to Violence .... page 23

Prayer 24 Prayer for Parent(s) with a Son or Daughter
in Prison .... page 24

Prayer 25 Prayer for Parent(s) with a Son or Daughter
in School or College .... page 25

Prayer 26 Prayer for Parent(s) Caring for a Son or Daughter
with Special-Needs or an Elder .... page 26

Prayer 27 Prayer for Parent(s) Dealing with a Difficult
Child or Teenager .... page 27

Prayer 28 Prayer of Hope for Those Who are Incarcerated .. page 28

Prayer 29 Prayer for My Community and the Poor .... page 29

Prayer 30 Prayer for Our Government and Those
in Authority .... page 30

Prayer 31 Prayer for the World .... page 31

Prayer 1

Prayer of Affirmation of Who I Am

So in Christ Jesus you are all children of God through faith. (Galatians 3: 26)

Father,

I thank You that You are God, the great I AM *(Exodus 3:14)*.

Thank You that You created me in Your image and likeness *(Genesis 1:26)*.

Thank You, that by faith, I am Your child *(Galatians 4:7)*.

Thank You for being my Father and that I can talk with You at any time.

I pray that You will continue to help me as You affirm who I am.

In Jesus' name, Amen.

Prayer for Salvation

If you declare with your mouth, "Jesus is Lord," and believe in your heart that God raised him from the dead, you will be saved. (Romans 10:9, NKJV)

Father,

I come to You my God and Lord *(Psalm 5:2)*, desiring to be saved from all of my sins.

I confess and repent of my current and past sins, and ask for Your forgiveness, in the name of Jesus.

I accept Jesus as my Lord and Savior.

I believe that He died on the cross for my sins, and that He rose from the grave on the third day.

Thank You, Father, for the gift of Salvation.

In Jesus' name, Amen.

Prayer to Increase One's Faith

You can never please God without faith, without depending on him. Anyone who wants to come to God must believe that there is a God and that he rewards those who sincerely look for him. (Hebrews 11:6, TLB)

✝

My Father in Heaven,

I praise and worship You.

I thank You for your great glory.

I know that all things are possible with You *(Matthew 19:26)*.

Your word says that it is impossible to please You without faith.

From the Old Testament to the New,
You show how great men and women walked by faith,
and achieved great things *(Hebrews 11)*.

I pray that You will increase my faith.

In Jesus' name, Amen.

Prayer 4

Prayer to Cease from Lying, Stealing or Other Wrongdoings

Submit yourselves, then, to God. Resist the devil, and he will flee from you. Come near to God and he will come near to you. Wash your hands, you sinners, and purify your hearts, you double-minded. (James 4:7-8)

✝

Lord, God of the Universe *(Psalm 89:11; Isaiah 42:5)*,

Who loves me *(Jeremiah 31:3)* and is always willing to give me second chances,

I confess my sins of lying, stealing, _____.

I repent of my sins and ask for your forgiveness.

Whenever I decide to stop doing these acts, I feel the urge to do them.

I pray that You will help me and give me the strength to resist the devil.

I submit my entire life to You now, desiring to draw closer to You and overcome my sins of _____.

In Jesus' name, Amen.

Prayer of Forgiveness

If we confess our sins, He is faithful and just to forgive us our sins and to cleanse us from all unrighteousness. (1 John 1:9, NKJV)

✝

Father,

I thank You that I can call You Father.

I come before you because You are all that I need *(Philippians 4:19).*

I bring my problems before You, knowing that even before I tell You of them, You know them *(Psalm 139:4).*

I confess and repent of bitterness and unforgiveness that I have harbored in my heart toward others.

I pray now, for Your forgiveness.

In Jesus' name, Amen.

Prayer to Love Others

This is the first and greatest commandment. The second most important is similar: 'Love your neighbor as much as you love yourself.' (Matthew 22:38-39, TLB)

---†---

Holy God *(Psalm 99:5),*

I thank You for Your unconditional love for me *(Jeremiah 31:3).*

I confess and repent that I have not
loved others as myself.

I pray God, that Your love will inspire me to love others.

In Jesus' name, Amen.

Prayer 7

Prayer to Overcome Fear

For the Spirit God gave us does not make us timid, but gives us power, love and self-discipline. (2 Timothy 1:7)

✝

God Almighty,

Creator of Heaven and Earth *(Isaiah 42:5)*,

You are King of Kings and Lord of Lords *(1 Timothy 6:15)*.

Thank You for inviting me to Your throne of grace.

I confess, repent, and renounce all manner of fears, such as fear of what others think of me, fear of the dark, fear of traveling over bridges, fear of death, fear of _____ *(include your own prayer here)*, and fear of going to the next level in my life.

I pray and ask for Your help in overcoming fear.

In Jesus' name, Amen.

Prayer to Overcome Jealousy or Gossip

But if we walk in the light as He is in the light, we have fellowship with one another, and the blood of Jesus Christ His Son cleanses us from all sin. (1 John1:7, NKJV)

✝

O Merciful God *(2 Corinthians 1:3)*,

I come to You, Lord God, because You are a just God *(Psalm 7:11)*, and worthy to be praised.

I confess and repent of jealousy and gossip.

I pray God that You will remind me that when I feel tempted to gossip or to be jealous of others, that I am not walking in the light, and that Your blood has already cleansed me from these acts.

I pray for Your help, Lord, in overcoming jealousy and gossip.

In Jesus' name, Amen.

Prayer to Overcome Anger or Guilt

If you are angry, don't sin by nursing your grudge. Don't let the sun go down with you still angry— get over it quickly. (Ephesians 4:26, TLB)

...let us go right in to God himself, with true hearts fully trusting him to receive us because we have been sprinkled with Christ's blood to make us clean and because our bodies have been washed with pure water. (Hebrews 10:22, TLB)

✝

God,

You are in the highest, and all glory belongs to You *(Luke 2:14)*.

I thank You, Father, for your greatness, and for Your peace that passes all understanding *(Philippians 4:7)*.

I confess, repent, and renounce my feelings of anger and guilt.

I ask for Your forgiveness, my God.

I pray, that I will no longer harbor anger and guilt in my heart.

Rather, I will draw near to You and trust You.

In Jesus' name, Amen.

Prayer 10

Prayer for Healing

... who forgives all your sins and heals all your diseases.
(Psalm 103:3)

✝

Father,

You are the God of comfort *(2 Corinthians 1:3)*.

You forgive all sins and heal all diseases.

I repent of every known and unknown sin that I have harbored.

I pray that You will forgive me of my wrongdoings.

I pray God, that you will heal me of sadness over _____ *(include the reason here)*.

I pray for healing of _____
(include your own prayer here).

I accept this healing by faith.

I thank You for my healing in Jesus' name, Amen.

Prayer 11

Prayer to Overcome Procrastination

I can do all things through Christ who strengthens me.
(Philippians 4:13, NKJV)

✝

Father,

There is nothing too hard for You.

I love You, my Creator and my Lord *(Isaiah 45:18)*.

I bring my issue of procrastination before You, because You are a God of love.

You have given me time on this earth and I plan to utilize it for your glory.

I thank You that You have given me zeal to move forward, and remain busy till You come.

I pray that You will eradicate procrastination from my life.

In Jesus' name, Amen.

Prayer 12

Prayer to Overcome My Past

...and from Jesus Christ who faithfully reveals all truth to us. He was the first to rise from death, to die no more. He is far greater than any king in all the earth. All praise to him who always loves us and who set us free from our sins by pouring out his lifeblood for us. (Revelation 1:5, TLB)

☦

Loving Father,

I know that You have washed away my sins, and that You no longer remember them *(Isaiah 43:25)*.

However, I continually think of my past wrongdoings and they have become stumbling blocks, preventing me from moving forward.

I pray that You will help me to overcome _____ *(include those areas here)*.

In Jesus' name, Amen.

Prayer 13

Prayer when Experiencing Anxiety, Loneliness, and Self-Pity

Cast all your anxiety on him because he cares for you.
(1 Peter 5:7)

Dear God,

Thank You that You are the God of comfort *(2 Corinthians 1:3)*.

I thank You because You are faithful, loving and kind *(Deuteronomy 7:9; Jeremiah 31:3)*.

God, I am experiencing anxiety about my life, and because I feel lonely, I have allowed self-pity to enter my mind.

I pray, Father, that You will heal me of anxiety, loneliness and self-pity.

In Jesus' name, Amen.

Prayer 14

Prayer for My Spouse

For this reason a man will leave his father and mother and be united to his wife, and the two will become one flesh. This is a profound mystery—but I am talking about Christ and the church. However, each one of you also must love his wife as he loves himself, and the wife must respect her husband. (Ephesians 5:31-33)

✝

Father,

I thank you for blessing me with my spouse_____ *(include spouse's name here).*

Thank you that he or she is supportive.

I pray that I will continue to love my spouse _____, and respect _____ him or her according to your word.

I pray also, that I will learn to communicate with him or her in a peaceful manner.

I pray Father, that You will heal my spouse of _____ and help him or her to overcome_____.

In Jesus' name, Amen.

Prayer 15

Prayer of Repentance

Don't you realize how patient he is being with you? Or don't you care? Can't you see that he has been waiting all this time without punishing you, to give you time to turn from your sin? His kindness is meant to lead you to repentance. (Romans 2:4 TLB)

✝

God,

Holy is your name *(Psalm 99:5)*.

I praise and worship You, God.

Thank You for your goodness Holy God.

I thank you that your goodness leads me to repentance.

I pray that You will continually lead me to repentance.

In Jesus' name, Amen.

Prayer 16

Prayer for Protection While Traveling

Whoever dwells in the shelter of the Most High will rest in the shadow of the Almighty. (Psalm 91:1)

✝

God of love *(Jeremiah 31:3)*,

thank You for Your love poured out just for me.

You show Your love to me by your presence.

Wherever I go, You are always there *(Psalm 139:7-14)*.

Yet, I worry when I am traveling either on a plane or over a bridge.

I pray for Your protection while traveling.

In Jesus' name, Amen.

Prayer for Wisdom and Understanding

And Jesus said to them, "I am the bread of life. He who comes to Me shall never hunger, and he who believes in Me shall never thirst. (John 6:35, NKJV)

God of Wisdom and Understanding *(Jeremiah 10:12)*,

I lift You up Father, and I magnify your name.

Thank You for imparting Your wisdom and understanding to me at home, in my community, or wherever I go.

I pray that You will continue to pour out Your wisdom and understanding in my heart, so I can help others.

In Jesus' name, Amen.

Prayer to Be Successful in Leadership

Now we can come fearlessly right into God's presence, assured of his glad welcome when we come with Christ and trust in him. (Ephesians 3:12, TLB)

✝

Father,

You sent Your Son to be Savior of the world *(John 17:3)*.

You gave Him boldness and confidence, even to go to the cross and die for my sins *(Romans 5:8)*.

Father, You are the God of leadership and success. You were successful when You created this world *(Isaiah 42:5)*.

I pray that You will impart Your wisdom to me, so that I can become a successful leader.

In Jesus' name, Amen.

Prayer 19

Prayer for a Single Parent

No, in all these things we are more than conquerors through him who loved us. (Romans 8.37)

✝

Magnificent God,

God of strength *(Psalm 28:7)*, I am a single Parent, needing finances, strength and peace, as I deal with my children.

I pray that You will help me to be a conqueror.

In Jesus' name, Amen.

Prayer for Patience While Seeking a Job

And my God shall supply all your need according to His riches in glory by Christ Jesus. (Philippians 4:19, NKJV)

✝

My God,

Who owns the cattle on a thousand hills *(Psalm 50:10)*, I praise you and thank You for giving me patience and strength *(Psalm 28:7)* as I seek a new job.

I pray Lord, that you will supply all my need, by furnishing me with the appropriate job and pay.

In Jesus' name, Amen.

Prayer for Healing from Drinking, Smoking or Drugs

For we are not fighting against people made of flesh and blood, but against persons without bodies - the evil rulers of the unseen world, those mighty satanic beings and great evil princes of darkness who rule this world; and against huge numbers of wicked spirits in the spirit world. (Ephesians 6:12, TLB)

For he has rescued us out of the darkness and gloom of Satan's kingdom and brought us into the Kingdom of his dear Son. (Colossians 1:13, TLB)

✝

God of light *(1 John 1:5)*,

I thank you, for in you, there is no darkness.

I bring my life-issues to you. I have been participating in _____ *(fill in a problematic area of your life)*.

I desire to change my life, Lord God. I confess, repent, and renounce _____, and ask for Your forgiveness, deliverance, and healing from_____.

I submit to You God and trust You for my life.

In Jesus' name, Amen.

Prayer 22

Prayer for an Individual Dealing with Bipolar, Schizophrenia, Anorexia, Bulimia and Other Disorders

See, I lay a stone in Zion, a chosen and precious cornerstone, and the one who trusts in him will never be put to shame. (1 Peter 2:6)

✝

Faithful and loving God,

Comforter of the Afflicted, I know that You love me regardless of my condition.

You desire that I trust You in all situations, that I submit to You, and bathe in Your glory.

I confess, repent, and ask for Your forgiveness for the anger, guilt, abandonment, unforgiveness, and other issues that I have harbored from my past, and that have contributed to my mental difficulties.

I pray that You will heal my broken heart and help me to believe in You.

I pray that You will heal me of_____
(include your disorder here).

In Jesus' name, Amen

Prayer for Parent(s) Who Lost a Son or Daughter to Violence

But may the God of all grace, who called us to His eternal glory by Christ Jesus, after you have suffered a while, perfect, establish, strengthen, and settle you. (1 Peter 5:10, NKJV)

✝

God of all grace and mercy *(2 John 3)*,

You are my burden-bearer *(Psalm 68:19)* and my Comforter *(2 Corinthians 1:3)*.

You continue to carry and comfort me throughout my time of grief, when I lost _____ *(include the name of your loved one here)* to violence.

Thank You, Lord God, that when I am weak, You are strong *(2 Corinthians 12:10)*. I pray, Lord, for Your continued strength and peace.

In Jesus' name, Amen.

Prayer 24

Prayer for Parent(s) with a Son or Daughter in Prison

... for every child of God can obey him, defeating sin and evil pleasure by trusting Christ to help him. (1 John 5:4, TLB)

✝

God,

Who is able to do exceedingly more than we think or imagine *(Ephesians 3:20)*, I thank you for your comfort as I grapple with the pain of knowing that my son or daughter _____ is in prison.

Thank You for the victory that overcomes the world *(1 John 5:4)*.

Thank You for being my overcomer *(John 16:33)*.

I pray that You will help me keep my faith alive, as I wait on my son's or daughter's release.

In Jesus' name, Amen.

Prayer 25

Prayer for Parent(s) with a Son or Daughter in School or College

He will cover you with his feathers and under his wings you will find refuge; his faithfulness will be your shield and rampart. (Psalm 91:4)

†

Almighty God,

You are my shelter in the time of storms.

I read every day of calamities taking place in schools, colleges, churches, synagogues and other places, where innocent people are at risk and many have been victims of violence.

Father, I pray for safety, not only for my sons and daughters, but for all people who may be at risk.

I pray that the power of Jesus' blood will protect and cover everyone.

In Jesus' name, Amen.

Prayer for Parent(s) Caring for a Son or Daughter with Special Needs or an Elder

And let us not grow weary while doing good, for in due season we shall reap if we do not lose heart. (Galatians 6:9, NKJV)

✝

Gracious God,

I magnify You. I praise You for the many years of strength and hope that You have given me, as I care for my special-needs son or daughter _____ *(include a name here),* or as I care for my elderly relative _____ *(include a name here).*

God, You have been good, kind, faithful, and wonderful *(Psalm 109:21; 1 Corinthians 1:9).*

I love You because You first loved me *(1 John 4:19).*

I pray that You will continually strengthen me, and give me hope and peace.

In Jesus' name, Amen.

Prayer 27

Prayer for Parent(s) Dealing with a Difficult Child or Teenager

Teach a child to choose the right path, and when he is older, he will remain upon it. (Proverbs 22:6, TLB)

God,

You are King of Kings and Lord of Lords *(1 Timothy 6:15)*.

I bless You and magnify You, for Your great glory and might *(Psalm 24:8)*.

I thank You, that Your word says to train up a child in the way he should go, so that when the child is old, he or she will not depart from it.

It has been difficult dealing with my son's or daughter's or grandchild's _____ *(include a name here)* rebellion.

I confess that if I have been enabling him/her, I pray that You will give me wisdom to train this child or teenager in the way he or she should go.

In Jesus' name, Amen.

Prayer 28

Prayer of Hope for Those Who Are Incarcerated

"Very truly I tell you, whoever hears my word and believes him who sent me has eternal life and will not be judged but has crossed over from death to life." (John 5:24)

✝

God of love,

Your Word shows me how to live *(Matthew 4:4)*, and how to change my way of life.

I confess and repent regarding the way that I have lived.

I am in prison, not sure if I will get another chance at life. However, You promised God, that if anyone believes in Jesus, and accepts Him as Lord and Savior, that he or she will have everlasting life and shall not come under condemnation.

I thank You for giving me the surety of everlasting life.

I submit to You Father and believe that Your Son, Jesus, died to give me life and to free me from condemnation.

I pray that I will have a chance at life again. I pray for the hope of eternal life when I can stand before Him and hear, "Well done" *(Matthew 25:21)*.

In Jesus' name, Amen.

Prayer for My Community and the Poor

He who has pity on the poor lends to the LORD. And He will pay back what he has given. (Proverbs 19:17, NKJV)

✝

God,

I pray that gun violence will cease in my community and people will live without fear, because Your word says that You have not given us a spirit of fear, but of power and love, and a sound mind.

I thank You that You care for the poor, including those who are homeless, hungry, and those who are in prison *(Psalm 68:10)*.

I thank You that everyone is accepted in Your sight *(Romans 2:11)*.

I pray that everyone will obtain salvation and live in unity.

I pray that everyone in communities will help those who are poor and destitute.

In Jesus' name, Amen.

Prayer for Our Government and Those in Authority

Obey the government, for God is the one who has put it there. There is no government anywhere that God has not placed in power. (Romans 13:1, TLB)

God over all
(1 Chronicles 29:11),

I pray for the government and those who have authority over us, that they will work to their full potential by providing policies to benefit the general populace including the poor among us.

Father I pray that You will give wisdom and understanding to the governing authorities, that they will govern in righteousness and provide justice for all.

I pray Father, that federal, state, and local governments will implement gun laws, in order to prevent individuals from killing innocent people.

In Jesus' name, Amen.

Prayer for the World

The earth is the LORD's, and everything in it, the world, and all who live in it; for he founded it on the seas and established it on the waters. (Psalm 24: 1-2).

✝

God of heaven and earth *(Isaiah 42:5)*,

You who founded the world and all who live in it,
I magnify You; I bless and glorify You. I thank You for Your greatness and Your mighty power. Thank You that You own everything in the world *(1 Chronicles 29:11)*.

I pray that people will have peace wherever they go. I pray for unity and love throughout the world. I pray for the poor and those in need that they will have food, clothing, shelter and clean water.

I also pray that those who are imprisoned without a just cause will be set free. I pray that all will know that Jesus lives, and that they can have salvation through Him. I pray that as I walk through this earth, I will be mindful that the world is Yours.

In Jesus' name, Amen.

Books Written by the Author

Standing on His Promises:
Finding Comfort, Hope, and Purpose in the Midst of Your Storm

Prayer and Meditation:
Finding Comfort, Hope, and Purpose in the Midst of Your Storm

Prayer and Meditation for Teens:
Finding Comfort, Hope, and Purpose in the Midst of Your Storm

Prayer and Meditation: Biblical Self-Help Tools for Parents of Teens When You Do Not Know Where to Turn

Rise Up: How to Overcome Your Battles Utilizing Faith and Belief in God

Gentle Breeze: Finding Comfort, Hope, and Purpose in the Midst of Your Storm

Contact us! We would love to hear from you:
WEB: Keytolifepublishingcompany.com
EMAIL: admin@keytolifepublishingcompany.com

Key to Life Publishing Company
P.O. Box 190971
Boston, MA 02119

Like us on Facebook:
Facebook.com/keytolifepublishingcompany

WEB: Keytolifeblog.com
EMAIL: joan@keytolifeblog.com

www.ingramcontent.com/pod-product-compliance
Lightning Source LLC
Chambersburg PA
CBHW030604020526
44112CB00048B/1246